M000166568

"No more wracking of your brain to look for the right questions to ask. Choon Seng has condensed the multitude of questions that readers can ask in almost every situation into this great little book. Solutions lie in the powerful questions we ask. This is a useful 'arsenal' for both new and experienced coaches, managers, leaders, and in fact anyone, for asking great questions to help others find the answers they seek."—**Trevor Chua, Assistant Director, Healthcare Leadership College, MOH Holdings Pte Ltd**

"Choon Seng is indeed a master coach! Having had the privilege to learn from him, I wish I could have his 'questions bank' to tap into whenever I coach my staff and my clients. With this book, now I can! I am sure you will find this book a great resource. Whether you are a manager needing to coach your people, or an executive coach working with your clients, or just a parent wanting to develop your children, this book is a gem to have."—**Christopher Tan, Chief Executive Officer, Providend Ltd**

"Choon Seng is a pioneer in the field of Action Learning. His wisdom and insights are captured in his very practical book about asking powerful questions!"—**Chuck Appleby, PhD, President, Appleby & Associates, LLC**

"What's Your Question? is a remarkable resource for anyone acting in a 'helping' role (i.e., facilitator, coach, leader, manager, consultant) who wants to truly empower their colleagues or teams. Often, finding the right question is the hardest part of empowering others. So to have this highly useful book organised into specific categories makes it extremely easy to find just the right question for any person at the right time. Without question, a best leadership practice is asking more and better questions to pivot the conversation."—**Thomas G. Crane, Author of *The Heart of Coaching,* President of Crane Consulting**

"Choon Seng is a master coach who not only grasps quickly the challenges an individual or organisation currently faces, but also, being certified in Emergenetics, respects his audience's diversity in thinking and behaviour, and has the ability to harness it. This book is testament to what he does best—asking questions that inspire great learning. His book sets the reader thinking through real-life critical questions, allowing the learner to reflect and apply directly to their own situations. This book is a wonderful companion to business leaders, coaches and facilitators—anyone who wants to change the status quo for the better."—**Terence Quek, Chief Executive Officer, Emergenetics International-Asia Pacific**

"As every WIAL Action Learning coach knows, curious and concise questions help one get to the root of an issue rapidly. Choon Seng has done an amazing job formulating these curious and concise questions that will be invaluable to not only Action Learning teams and coaches, but to problem-solvers the world over."—**Dr. Bea Carson, President, World Institute for Action Learning (WIAL)**

"In today's context, it is NOT what you know that is important, it is knowing what you do NOT know that is key to making effective decisions. This book is an essential primer on what are the absolute key questions that should be discussed (and not assumed) around the table. This book does not promise answers, but rather promises useful conversations that could lead to new answers and possibilities for consideration."—**Raizan bin Abdul Razak, Assistant Director, PS21 and Culture, Organisation Development Division**

"The questions in this book form a powerful toolkit, which can be used by coaches, managers or business leaders to increase the impact of the work they do. Organised by competencies and leadership situations, the questions help the reader get to the heart of many common leadership situations."—**Shannon Banks, Managing Director, Be Leadership Ltd**

"*What's Your Question?* is an invaluable, practical, and easy-to-use guide for applying and benefiting from the power of questions in thinking and communicating. The reader needs only to ask 'What do I want my question to accomplish?' and then search in the book to discover the category of questions that will provide the most help. I highly recommend *What's your Question?* as an essential and powerful guide for any professional."—**Marilee Adams, PhD, Best-selling author of *Change Your Questions, Change Your Life***

"If you are a teacher facing a class of non-responsive pupils, or a facilitator running a workshop with participants who are unfamiliar with one another, or a manager chairing a meeting with your unmotivated staff, or a sales representative dealing with a client whose wallet can only be prised open with a crowbar, or a parent trying to communicate with teenage children whose only responses are 'Don't know' and 'Who cares', or simply someone who is keen to learn from the people and situations around him or her—then this book is for you! This book will be a perfect companion to help you ask the right questions, depending on your situation and purpose."—**Prakash Nair, Associate Trainer, Civil Service College**

"Asking a question is arguably the simplest skill since childhood. But asking the right question at the right moment is an art that needs constant honing. This book provides you with a tool bag of suggested and ready questions, both for different competencies and situations. From my practical experience, these questions are appropriately crafted to solicit the right response, be it to validate a certain understanding, stimulate discussion or elicit deeper insights during day-to-day conversations, formal meetings or even performance reviews."—**Lieutenant Colonel Alvin Chia, Head, Centre for Army Lessons Learnt, Singapore Army (2010-2013)**

"This book should be a reference book in every Action Learning coaches' library. A key skill that every Action Learning coach needs to master is how to convert observations of sub-optimising team behaviour into questions that will foster reflection and change in individual and team behaviours. Choon Seng has done a masterful job in creating useful questions that are key to team and leadership competencies and situations that Action Learning teams frequently encounter."—**Skipton Leonard, PhD, Managing Director, Learning Thru Action LLC**

"Solutions are often found in the questions asked. Effective leaders ask insightful questions and this is certainly a good resource guide for leaders and managers to kick start the process of empowering staff to think more critically about issues and challenges through the use of questions. I would recommend all leaders to get a copy of this book and think about *What's Your Question?* for your solution."—**Dr. Timothy Low, Chief Executive Officer, Farrer Park Hospital**

"With this book, you can find a shortcut to master a great skill, which is the ability to ask a great question at the right time, so that you can learn more and move things forward. With this useful toolkit, you do not need to waste time searching for good questions anymore."—**Simon Kuang, Senior Consultant, K.S Consulting**

"As an executive coach, we are trained to ask 'powerful' questions. This is a timely, practical, and useful book, not just for us coaches, but for anyone who subscribes to the belief that we learn much more from asking and active listening (with the intent to understand, then respond) than talking. Having been a coach for close to two decades, I have just acquired an additional resource to add to my pursuit in impactful coaching."—**Paul Heng, Executive Coach, NeXT Consulting Group**

"*What's Your Question?* is the answer to many leaders', facilitators' and coaches' search for a good book on questions. Choon Seng's approach on questions from the competency and situation dimensions is unique for it interweaves both theory and practice from his work in helping individuals, teams, and organisations."—**William Teo, Country Director, World Institute for Action Learning (WIAL) – Malaysia**

"What if we can find the right questions every time we need them? How do we start asking questions that work well in different situations? What if there is a book that can help us be more natural at asking questions? Guess what? You are holding that book in your hands right now. What are you waiting for? Enjoy the journey of transforming your life through questions!"—**Faz Kamaruddin, Head of Performance, Talent and Development, AirAsia**

"One of the most common questions I hear is 'How can I get better at asking questions?' Well, Choon Seng is a master of questions and this book provides us with an amazing buffet of questions to ponder on. For just about every context imaginable, this book offers food for thought and inquiry. So if you are a person who would like to enhance your questioning skills, how about jumping into this excellent resource to expand your range of questions?"—**Dr. Douglas O'Loughlin, Senior**

"This book is a valuable gift to anyone who thinks: 'I wish I could ask great questions.' If you have ever experienced being 'stuck' in a situation, the contents of this book will help you manage better the next time. If you are a manager or practitioner who works with people, these questions can add to your toolkit in creating engaging conversations with your folks in stretching their thinking and performance. I would recommend that you use this with your teams, to nudge them toward an inquiring culture, triggering reflection, appreciation, learning, and innovation."—**Jayan Warrier, Director, Performance Solutions, Positive Performance Consulting Pte Ltd**

"Whether you are a facilitator, trainer, manager, coach, teacher, interviewer or negotiator, this book provides a useful reference for anyone who is seeking to improve their questioning skills. The book contains a compilation of questions based on 45 competencies and situations. Some are short, but sharp questions designed to get quickly to the heart of the matter. Others are questions designed to provoke deeper, reflective thinking. All are conveniently organised by competency and situation. With space to provide personal additions and reflections, this book is highly practical and will become a valuable resource on your bookshelf."—**Lindsay Sumner, CPF, Managing Director, Bank House Associates Ltd**

"This is the first book I know of that contains so many useful questions classified by topics to help Action Learning coaches and leaders. As an Action Learning coach, I always notice the struggle of participants, especially during the first few sessions, to ask what we call 'great questions'. This book also reflects the very long, wide, and deep experience of the author."—**Dr. Daniel Belet, Co-founder of World Institute for Action Learning (WIAL) – France**

"Asking good or even great questions can be challenging during coaching sessions or in any other situations for that matter. It requires perseverance to continue asking questions until we have the ability to ask good questions. This book helps to make asking questions easier and will be useful to anyone!"—**Rafidah Bte Suparman, Ex-Superintendent of Changi Women's Prison**

"It is said that 'All change begins with a question', and that 'Life = Change'. I am so happy that Choon Seng has written this book to guide me and many more change practitioners in the important work of creating better results for ourselves and our clients."—**Marisol D. Lopez, Chairman of World Institute for Action Learning (WIAL) – Philippines, Co-founder of Society for Organisational Learning (Philippines), President of The Rizal Academy for Innovation and Leadership**

"Once leaders have discovered the power of asking questions, they often struggle to actually apply this seemingly basic skill. They ask: 'But how do I go about creating great questions?' Great questions depend on the situation and context, and are therefore extremely varied. Choon Seng has created a very practical guide to offer powerful sample questions for 45 different situations and focus areas. These questions will help leaders start a meaningful conversation and gradually build their confidence and skill in asking questions to solve problems and develop their teams."—**Peter Cauwelier, PhD, Team Coach, ASIO Consulting**

"There is an abundance of literature convincing us of the power of questions. Harnessing this power starts from knowing what questions to ask. Good questions help expand our capacity for learning and the discovery of new insights. Good questions help develop a team's shared understanding and expand their capacity for co-creation. This is a timely resource by Choon Seng, drawing upon his extensive experience as a practitioner in action learning and facilitation. It is a handy guide for anyone who is ready to relearn the art of asking good questions and recapture the childlike curiosity we used to have."—**Dr. Yee Lai Fong, Ed.D. (The George Washington University), Organisational Learning Specialist**

"As a facilitator, I find this book useful in its very comprehensive coverage of competencies and situations. I see its immediate use as a good starter to ask ourselves, and our teams, good questions. The book also invites us to reflect on the lenses we use when asking questions. The lists of questions, succinct at seven questions per category, thus provide a scaffold for us to formulate even more questions."—**Low Ming Hwee, Lead, Organisation Development in Public Sector Hospital**

"In this book, I realised that there is still a world of opportunities to facilitate deeper and more meaningful conversations in all of my clients' engagements. *What's Your Question?* conveniently puts into our hands the seeds of such conversations to help us attain higher levels of questioning skill."— **Cristina Alafriz, Partner & Senior Consultant, Management Strategies**

"In the modern society, many are looking for answers. However, the key is in asking questions. Through questions, we direct our search for answers. Sometimes, the question will point us to search for an answer in a different direction from where we initially planned to go. This book is a very useful compilation of questions that many have been searching for."—**Lye Yen Kai, CPF, Managing Director, Pivotal Learning Pte Ltd**

First published April 2016

Candid Creation Publishing books are available through most major bookstores in Singapore. For bulk order of our books at special quantity discounts, please email us at enquiry@candidcreation.com

What's Your Question?
Inspiring Possibilities through the Power of Questions

Author   : Ng Choon Seng
Publisher   : Phoon Kok Hwa
Editor   : Dewgem Yen
Layout   : Corrine Teng
Illustrations : Wendy Wong
Cover design: Ryanne Ng
Published by : Candid Creation Publishing LLP
                167 Jalan Bukit Merah,
                Connection One Tower 4, #06-12,
                Singapore 150167
Website   : www.candidcreation.com
Facebook   : Facebook/CandidCreationPublishing
Email   : enquiry@candidcreation.com
ISBN   : 978-981-09-9003-9

National Library Board, Singapore Cataloguing-in-Publication Data

Name(s): Ng, Choon Seng, 1967-
Title: What's your question? : inspiring possibilities through the power of questions / Ng Choon Seng.
Other title(s): Inspiring possibilities through the power of questions.
Description: Singapore : Candid Creation Publishing LLP, 2016.
Identifier(s): OCN 946060413 | ISBN 978-981-09-9003-9(paperback)

What's Your Question?

Inspiring Possibilities Through
The Power of Questions

Ng Choon Seng

CONTENTS

SITUATIONS

FOREWORD

Questions are powerful. Great questions have the ability to dramatically change ourselves and the world around us. They can solve complex problems, build relationships, create learning opportunities, and generate significant actions.

That is why I am so honoured and proud to write the Foreword for this wonderful book on questions written by Ng Choon Seng, my friend, professional colleague, and former student. In this book, Choon Seng has identified 630 great questions that will enable the reader to demonstrate needed competencies and handle numerous situations. These are questions that have been tested and honed over time and, I am sure, will lead to great results and success for the questioner. Choon Seng's questions have inspired me, and will hopefully excite and encourage you in using them in your day-to-day lives.

Both Choon Seng and I were encouraged by our parents to ask questions. We have also heard some of the best questions from our children. Questions have led the both of us to the wonderful world and methodology of action learning, a powerful questioning tool which is now being used by thousands of organisations around the world to develop leaders, build problem-solving teams, and

There is an axiom that states "Great leaders ask great questions". But the counter to that statement is also true: "Great questions help you become a great leader." As a professor in a global human resource development programme, I often tell my students that our programme will be successful if the student has more questions at the end of the programme as he or she had at the beginning. For questions are necessary for deep understanding and learning of any subject. It is even more important in examining one's life, for as Henry Thoreau wrote in Walden Pond: "An unexamined life is not worth living."

When asked to autograph my book, *Leading with Questions*, I always sign with the words "May your life be filled with great questions!" Anyone who is fortunate enough to live such a life will become a person with great wisdom, courage, passion, insight, and humility—someone who will make the world better for others. An unasked question may become a lost opportunity to serve others. May this book empower you to be someone who indeed is a great questioner.

Professor Michael Marquardt
George Washington University
Past President, World Institute for Action Learning

Many of us started asking questions from a young age and it stemmed simply from our curiosity of the world around us. Over time, it is not uncommon that we view questioning as something so fundamental and instinctive that we do not need to think about it. Unfortunately, as we grow up, most of us start asking fewer questions and making more statements. Instead of asking, we fall into the trap of assuming. Instead of asking questions freely, we start to hold back because we are afraid of asking the "wrong" questions.

This is a pity as good questions often invite people to open up about themselves and divulge their thoughts and feelings on a wide variety of topics. Questions also play a critical role in empowering people to innovate, solve problems, and move ahead in both their professional and personal lives.

Personally, I have to admit that I was not adept at asking questions in the past. My questioning skills only started improving after I met Choon Seng in 2010, when he introduced me to the beautiful world of action learning. I immediately fell in love with this problem-solving methodology and went on to pursue my certification as a Professional Action Learning Coach. Through action learning, I learnt to leverage on the power of questions to to develop leaders at the same time. Along this learning journey, I realised there was so much that I did not know about asking good questions.

Understanding the importance of raising questions and being able to ask good ones are two separate matters. Many people have great difficulty and spend considerable time thinking about or looking for suitable questions to ask in specific situations. It is also not easy for many people to ask questions that are focussed on specific competencies. But Choon Seng, whom I am indebted to as a mentor, has never ceased to amaze me with his repertoire of questions that works really effectively in helping individuals and groups make things happen. When he first revealed his intent to publish this book, I could not have been more pleased, because I know it will be a very valuable tool to many people.

It is my fervent hope that this quick reference guide will help minimise the amount of effort and time required of you to find or develop questions. Most importantly, I hope this book serves as a seed for you to *grow* more and better questions of your own, and start you on your journey to discovering the magic of questions.

Phoon Kok Hwa
Publisher

PREFACE

❝ The important thing is not to stop questioning. Curiosity has its own reason for existing. **❞**
Albert Einstein

In my younger days, I was often asked: "What's your question?" On more occasions than I can remember, I had difficulty coming up with questions that I felt were good. It did not help that I was not fond of asking questions either. I recall being lost in the U.S. many years ago and would rather fumble over maps (GPS was not commonly available then) than ask for directions at a nearby gas station. I am sure many of us have been caught in a similar situation before.

However, all that changed after I started to embark on my facilitation, organisational development and learning journey more than 25 years ago. Through the journey, I discovered that asking questions is one of the most important, if not the most important, interventions for learning. Whether we are business leaders, coaches, facilitators, meeting chairpersons, managers or even customers, we need to ask questions to help us learn better and inspire

In my professional learning journey, I have had the privilege of learning from many mentors from around the world. One of them is Dr. Michael Marquardt, Professor of Human Resource Development and International Affairs and Chairman of the Board of Advisors for the World Institute for Action Learning (WIAL). Dr. Marquardt is also the author of many leadership books, including the best-selling book, *Leading With Questions*. He has been instrumental to my growth as a Master Action Learning Coach (MALC). Through Dr. Marquardt and the WIAL Action Learning process, I have learnt to ask better questions in my professional and personal life. A piece of advice from Dr. Marquardt that has served me particularly well is:

"The seed of the solution lies in the question."

Often, we would also find that our questions are determined by the mindset we adopt. I am indebted to Dr. Marilee Adams for teaching me the Inquiry Mindset. She is the president and founder of Inquiry Institute, a consulting, coaching, and educational organisation, and the originator of the QUESTION THINKING™ methodologies. Her book, *Change Your Question, Change Your Life* inspired me to travel to Princeton in 2011 to become certified in her Question Thinking Advantage workshop.

me to ask questions from the learner's mindset, guided by the principle that changing our questions brings about changes to our results.

My best "question" teacher is actually my son, Titus. Over the years, he has asked me many questions born out of curiosity—questions that I did not have answers to. "Why is rough paper called rough paper?", "Why are bubbles round?", "Why is the police uniform blue?", "Does man become shorter in space?" and so forth. His burning curiosity serves as my impetus to learn more about questions and develop myself in this area.

In my interaction with other facilitators and coaches, I am frequently asked "How to ask questions?" and "What questions to ask?" Many have shared with me that questions seem to come to me rather naturally. These feedback got me thinking that perhaps I can support more individuals and teams by coming up with a book of questions that will trigger new insights.

HOW TO USE THIS BOOK

This book is a compilation of 630 questions that can be asked when focussing on different competencies or when in different situations. They serve as trigger questions to aid you in your quest to inspire more possibilities in whatever

Questions can be used to develop competencies in a particular area. For example, if you would like to focus on being forward looking, you can select questions under "Visioning" to develop yourself in that competency.

Questions are also powerful when you find yourself in situations that require you to ask different questions for the betterment of self, others, team, and organisation. For example, if your team is trying to solve a problem but is stuck, you can pick and ask a question under "Getting Unstuck" to help the team move forward.

All the questions in this book are not meant to be the right questions to ask in each context. They are only meant to help you kick start the questioning process. The questions need not be asked in the same sequence as they are listed too. Feel free to pick and choose any question that you feel will be useful at a particular point of time. More often than not, you will need to ask more follow-up questions after asking the one listed in the book.

This book also gives you the opportunity to expand your learning by being creative in the way you ask your questions. Feel free to rephrase the questions to suit different can be rephrased to "How can I do better?" if you wish to ask a self-reflective question. Or if you are working with a team, the question can be rephrased to "How can we do better as a team?"

The list of questions in each category is definitely not exhaustive and that is the reason why we have added blank lines for you to pen down your own questions. It is my fervent hope that in time to come, your list of questions will grow and so will your ability to ask good questions.

So have a go at experimenting with the questions to enrich your learning and discovery processes, and let us inspire more possibilities through the power of questions!

COMPETENCIES

1.

Accountability

#1   What are you accountable for?

#2   Who are you accountable to?

#3   How do we keep ourselves mutually accountable?

#4   What does accountability mean to you?

#5   How thorough is the research?

#6   Why is it not possible to do this?

#7   What does it take to do this?

#8 ....

....

#9 ....

....

#10 ....

....

#11 ....

....

#12 ....

4.

Appreciative Inquiry

#1 Can you describe a time when you were most proud of yourself? What happened? Who was involved? Why was it a proud moment?

#2 Is there a leader who inspires you? What made his leadership great? What did he do or not do? What inspired you?

#3 What have you accomplished in the past three years? How did it make you feel?

#4 What were the conditions that made you successful?

#5   What do you like about yourself, your department, or your organisation?

#6   What brings out the best in you?

#7   What are you grateful for in your life, career or organisation?

#8   ....

      ....

#9   ....

      ....

#10   ....

      ....

#11   ....

      ....

#12   ....

5.

Assertiveness

#1   Why are you afraid of asserting your views?

#2   How can you put your point across without diminishing the views of others?

#3   How can you develop your assertiveness?

#4   What small steps can you take to address your needs?

#5   What are the areas you can do more?

#6   What is the stretch goal?

#7   How satisfied are you with the results?

#8   ....

     ....

#9   ....

     ....

#10 ....

     ....

#11 ....

     ....

#12 ....

3.

Analytical Thinking

#1   What is the real issue?

#2   Why are you doing this?

#3   What is the purpose of doing this?

#4   What evidence or data do you have?

#5   What are the risks involved?

#6   What risks are we willing to take?

#7   How do we maximise our returns?

#8 ....

     ....

#9 ....

     ....

#10 ....

     ....

#11 ....

     ....

#12 ....

7.

Coaching

#1 What is your goal?

#2 What is your current situation?

#3 What are your options?

#4 What actions would you take?

#5   What would be your first few steps?

#6   Who can help you?

#7   How do you ensure success?

#8   ....

....

#9   ....

....

#10 ....

....

#11 ....

....

#12 ....

8.

Compassion

#1   What do you care about?

#2   What do you worry about?

#3   Who do you care about the most?

#4   How can I help you?

#5   How can you empathise with him?

#6   How can I be of service?

#7   What do you need right now?

#8   ....

     ....

#9   ....

     ....

#10 ....

     ....

#11 ....

     ....

#12 ....

9.

Conceptual Thinking

#1   What could be fun?

#2   What is the big picture?

#3   How can we be creative?

#4   Can we try something new?

#5   What is possible?

#6   How can we explore further?

#7   What other options are there?

#8   ....

      ....

#9   ....

      ....

#10   ....

      ....

#11   ....

      ....

#12   ....

10.

Conflict Management

#1 What are the issues at hand?

#2 What do we disagree on?

#3 How do we look for the third alternative?

#4 Can we find some common ground?

#5   How can we deal with the issue and not the person?

#6   How can we reach a "win-win" situation?

#7   What is the real issue behind the conflict?

#8   ....

....

#9   ....

....

#10 ....

....

#11 ....

....

#12 ....

11.

Courage

#1   How do I build courage?

#2   What are you afraid of?

#3   What is the worst thing that could happen?

#4   What could be the best result?

#5   Why are we not exercising courage?

#6   How can we be lion-hearted?

#7   How do I overcome my fears?

#8   ....

     ....

#9   ....

     ....

#10 ....

     ....

#11 ....

     ....

#12 ....

12. Creativity

#1 What crazy ideas can we think of?

#2 What happens if we do the exact opposite?

#3 How can this terrible idea be turned into a good idea?

#4 How can these ideas be combined to create a better solution?

#5   What happens if we decide that this is not a
      problem?

#6   What ideas would a six-year-old come up
      with?

#7   What is limiting our ideas?

#8   ....

      ....

#9   ....

      ....

#10   ....

      ....

#11   ....

      ....

#12   ....

13.

Critical Thinking

#1   What is the goal of it all?

#2   What evidence or data do we have/need?

#3   What is the real problem that we are trying to solve?

#4   Are we kidding ourselves?

#5   What assumptions are we making?

#6   Have we taken a deep and hard look at our
     situation?

#7   Did our proposed solution solve the problem
     we are facing?

#8   ....

     ....

#9   ....

     ....

#10 ....

     ....

#11 ....

     ....

#12 ....

14.

Customer Focus

#1   What do our customers need?

#2   Who are our customers?

#3   How much do we understand our customers?

#4   How do we build customer loyalty?

#5   Is everyone in the organisation focussing on the customers?

#6   What assumptions are we making about our customers?

#7   How do we leverage on our customers?

#8 ....

....

#9 ....

....

#10 ....

....

#11 ....

....

#12 ....

15.

Decision-Making

#1   Who or what would be affected by this decision?

#2   Who would be surprised by our decision?

#3   Is this the best decision that we can come up with?

#4   What are the ethical implications that come with this decision?

#5   Who needs to be involved in this?

#6   Is everyone agreeable to this decision?

#7   Can we sleep at night with this decision?

#8   ....

     ....

#9   ....

     ....

#10 ....

     ....

#11 ....

     ....

#12 ....

16.

Diversity

#1   How are we different from one another?

#2   How can we leverage diversity?

#3   What strengths can we harness from diversity?

#4   What differences do we need to manage?

#5 How do we take everyone's views into consideration?

#6 What is the best role for each individual?

#7 How do we ensure appreciation for one another?

#8 ....

....

#9 ....

....

#10 ....

....

#11 ....

....

#12 ....

17.

Drive for Results

#1   How do we ensure that the outcomes are achieved?

#2   What are our objectives?

#3   What needs to happen before we can achieve our goals?

#4   What must we do differently next time?

#5   Would the problem be solved after we implement this?

#6   What are the intangible outcomes?

#7   How do we know that we have achieved results?

#8 ....

....

#9 ....

....

#10 ....

....

#11 ....

....

#12 ....

18.

Empathy

#1　How can you see from his point of view?

#2　How can you understand his needs?

#3　How can you listen better without judging?

#4　What are his concerns?

#5 What are some of his struggles?

#6 How are our perspectives similar?

#7 How can I connect with him?

#8 ....

....

#9 ....

....

#10 ....

....

#11 ....

....

#12 ....

19.

Expressiveness

#1   Can you be the first person to speak up?

#2   Why are you holding back?

#3   What can you do to speak up freely?

#4   How can others benefit from the sharing of
     your viewpoint?

#5   What is your intention of sharing?

#6   How can you loosen up a little?

#7   How can we help you to speak up?

#8   ....

     ....

#9   ....

     ....

#10 ....

     ....

#11 ....

     ....

#12 ....

20.
Fairness

#1   Are you being fair?

#2   Am I being objective in this matter?

#3   What is an equitable outcome for all?

#4   How can you reach a fair decision for everyone?

#5 How do I meet everyone's needs?

#6 How can I be fair to myself?

#7 What does "fair" mean to you?

#8 ....

    ....

#9 ....

    ....

#10 ....

    ....

#11 ....

    ....

#12 ....

21.

Flexibility

#1 What would you lose if you changed this approach?

#2 What would you gain if you changed this approach?

#3 Would this change bring a better good for all?

#4 What am I afraid of the change?

#5   Is this a battle worth fighting?

#6   What should I be focussing on instead?

#7   What can you do to become more flexible?

#8   ....

....

#9   ....

....

#10 ....

....

#11 ....

....

#12 ....

22.
Humility

#1   Are we getting ahead of ourselves?

#2   How do we prevent ourselves from being
       overconfident?

#3   What happens if we forget our humble
       beginnings?

#4   What are the dangers of being prideful?

#5   Are we celebrating too early in the game?

#6   How does being humble help us?

#7   Are we taking things for granted?

#8   ....

....

#9   ....

....

#10 ....

....

#11 ....

....

#12 ....

23.

Inclusiveness

#1   Who are the stakeholders involved/impacted?

#2   Are there people whom we have left out?

#3   How do we ensure that we leave no one behind?

#4   How do we make use of everyone's talents?

#5   How do we embrace diversity?

#6   What can be done to get everyone involved?

#7   Do we know the strengths of each individual?

#8   ....

....

#9   ....

....

#10 ....

....

#11 ....

....

#12 ....

24.

Integrity

#1   Can we sleep at night with this decision?

#2   How honest have we been with ourselves?

#3   What are we hiding?

#4   What does this say about our integrity?

#5 Am I able to explain this to my children in future?

#6 Would we be able to hold our heads high after doing this?

#7 Who are we kidding?

#8 ....

....

#9 ....

....

#10 ....

....

#11 ....

....

#12 ....

25.

Listening

#1 On a scale of 1 to 10, how would you rate your listening skill?

#2 Are you listening to understand or listening to reply?

#3 What is the story behind what the person is saying?

#4 Am I listening or hearing?

#5   What are the ingredients of active listening?

#6   What happens if we do not listen?

#7   How does my judgement influence my
     listening?

#8   ....

     ....

#9   ....

     ....

#10 ....

     ....

#11 ....

     ....

#12 ....

26.

Motivation

#1   Do I know what motivates them?

#2   What are my motivations?

#3   How would they be motivated?

#4   If not now, then when?

#5   How can we take the first step?

#6   What would give you that satisfaction?

#7   What drives you?

#8 ....

....

#9 ....

....

#10 ....

....

#11 ....

....

#12 ....

27.

Negotiation

#1   What would cause a stalemate?

#2   What are my non-negotiables?

#3   When would I give in?

#4   What would make him accept?

#5   How far are you willing to go?

#6   Is this a battle worth fighting?

#7   How much do I want this?

#8   ....

....

#9   ....

....

#10 ....

....

#11 ....

....

#12 ....

28.

Open to Change

#1   What are you afraid of?

#2   How open are you to the change?

#3   What skills are needed to manage the change?

#4   What would help you embrace the change?

#5   What do you need?

#6   What will make the change easier to accept?

#7   What is the bright side to the change?

#8   ....

     ....

#9   ....

     ....

#10 ....

     ....

#11 ....

     ....

#12 ....

29.

Orientation to Details

#1   What is missing?

#2   What am I missing?

#3   What would I see or not see if I were to zoom in under a microscope?

#4   What are my blind spots?

#5 Who can help me spot my mistakes?

#6 Did you leave any stones unturned?

#7 How can I ensure that I do not miss out on anything?

#8 ....

....

#9 ....

....

#10 ....

....

#11 ....

....

#12 ....

30.

Patience

#1 Are you rushing to complete this?

#2 How can we slow down to move faster?

#3 What are the benefits of taking a step back?

#4 What are the dangers of rushing into this?

#5 How can the virtue of patience help us in this situation?

#6 How can we develop patience?

#7 Are you being overly patient in this situation?

#8 ....

....

#9 ....

....

#10 ....

....

#11 ....

....

#12 ....

31.

People Development

#1   What does he need to learn?

#2   How can he benefit from this?

#3   What kind of developmental activities would be helpful to him?

#4   How do we empower him to take charge of his own learning?

#5 Apart from sending him for courses, how else can he learn this?

#6 How would he apply what he has learnt?

#7 Who can he learn from?

#8 ....

    ....

#9 ....

    ....

#10 ....

    ....

#11 ....

    ....

#12 ....

32.

Perseverance

#1   How can you see this project to completion?

#2   What resources do you need to press on?

#3   Who can help you overcome this setback?

#4   How do you keep this sustainable?

#5   How do we find a booster for this?

#6   How do we evoke the "never-say-die" spirit?

#7   What would we say at our last breath?

#8   ....

      ....

#9   ....

      ....

#10   ....

      ....

#11   ....

      ....

#12   ....

33.

Project Management

#1   What are the objectives?

#2   What are our strategies and tasks?

#3   How should we measure our success?

#4   Are there other issues that could have an impact on the success of the project?

#5   What is our timeline?

#6   Where could things go wrong?

#7   What is our mitigation plan?

#8   ....

      ....

#9   ....

      ....

#10   ....

      ....

#11   ....

      ....

#12   ....

34.

Resilience

#1   How can I overcome this?

#2   What can I learn from this?

#3   Where/What do I draw strength from?

#4   What would I gain from all these?

#5   What would I do if I survived this?

#6   How do I press on?

#7   What would be my regret if I did not do this?

#8   ....

....

#9   ....

....

#10 ....

....

#11 ....

....

#12 ....

35.

Resource Management

#1   What are the available resources?

#2   What is our most valued resource?

#3   How do we maximise our resources?

#4   What can we do to make more with less?

#5 In what ways are we wasting our resources?

#6 What are our strengths?

#7 How can we manage our resources wisely?

#8 ....

....

#9 ....

....

#10 ....

....

#11 ....

....

#12 ....

36.

Risk-Taking

#1   What is the worst thing that can happen?

#2   What is the best result that can be achieved from this?

#3   Can you imagine the possibilities if we were to do this?

#4   What if you had no choice?

#5 How can you use your strengths to mitigate the risks?

#6 Is a small chance better than no chance?

#7 How can you mitigate some of the risks?

#8 ....

....

#9 ....

....

#10 ....

....

#11 ....

....

#12 ....

37.
Self-Development

#1   What are my strengths?

#2   What are my weaknesses?

#3   How can I be more deliberate in using more
      of my strengths?

#4   Who or what can help me?

#5   What am I afraid of?

#6   How can I be a better person?

#7   How would the world be better with a better me?

#8   ....

     ....

#9   ....

     ....

#10 ....

     ....

#11 ....

     ....

#12 ....

38.

Self-
Reflection

#1   Why did I think that way?

#2   Where was I coming from?

#3   Who was I trying to be?

#4   Why did I say what I said?

#5   What caused me to be so upset? Which values
      were compromised?

#6   What are my fears?

#7   What do I really want?

#8 ....

....

#9 ....

....

#10 ....

....

#11 ....

....

#12 ....

39.

Social Thinking

#1　How are we feeling right now?

#2　Who is involved in this?

#3　How can we work together?

#4　How do we get people to be connected with this?

#5   What do we care about?

#6   Who would benefit from this?

#7   How can you make a difference?

#8   ....

     ....

#9   ....

     ....

#10 ....

     ....

#11 ....

     ....

#12 ....

40.

Strategic Thinking

#1 What are the long-term goals?

#2 Where do we see ourselves five years from now?

#3 What is the big picture?

#4 What sort of culture do we want to create?

#5   What is most important to us?

#6   How does this support our goals?

#7   Are we missing the forest for the trees?

#8   ....

     ....

#9   ....

     ....

#10 ....

     ....

#11 ....

     ....

#12 ....

41.

Structural Thinking

#1   What are the steps to do this?

#2   What is the plan?

#3   How do we know we have reached our goal?

#4   What are the systems and structures?

#5 What is the timeline?

#6 Have you thought of the contingencies?

#7 What have we missed?

#8 ....

    ....

#9 ....

    ....

#10 ....

    ....

#11 ....

    ....

#12 ....

42. Systems Thinking

#1 How are they connected?

#2 What is the bigger picture?

#3 What is the impact if we were to do this?

#4 Is there only one solution to a problem?

#5 What kind of problems would this solution create?

#6 How are you involved in this?

#7 How are these issues correlated?

#8 ....

....

#9 ....

....

#10 ....

....

#11 ....

....

#12 ....

43.

Teamwork

#1 How do you build teamwork?

#2 What are the components of great teamwork?

#3 How do you leverage on the strengths of every team member?

#4 Which stage of team development is the team at?

#5　How can the team foster greater teamwork?

#6　How do you sustain great teamwork?

#7　On a scale of 1 to 10, how well are we performing as a team?

#8　...

....

#9　...

....

#10 ....

....

#11 ....

....

#12 ....

44.

Trust

#1   How do we build trust?

#2   Why is trust so important?

#3   How do we define trust?

#4   Is trust more important than anything else?

#5   What happens if trust is lost?

#6   How do you maintain trust?

#7   How do we improve our trustworthiness?

#8 ....

....

#9 ....

....

#10 ....

....

#11 ....

....

#12 ....

Visioning

#1   What is our vision?

#2   How do we envisage our future?

#3   Is this the future we want?

#4   What would everyone be saying about us in future?

#5   What inspires you about the vision?

#6   If there were one thing you can change about
     the future, what would it be?

#7   How can we create a shared vision?

#8   ....

     ....

#9   ....

     ....

#10 ....

     ....

#11 ....

     ....

#12 ....

SITUATIONS

1.

Addressing the Elephant in the Room

#1   What are we refusing to see?

#2   What is preventing us from talking about the real issue?

#3   Does everyone see the elephant in the room?

#4   Why are we not addressing the real issue?

#5 What must happen in order for us to talk about the elephant in the room?

#6 What are we avoiding in our conversations?

#7 Is there an elephant in the room? What do you think it is?

#8 ....

....

#9 ....

....

#10 ....

....

#11 ....

....

#12 ....

2.
Application
of Ideas

#1   What can we learn from this?

#2   How do we apply what we have learnt?

#3   How would this work for us?

#4   How can we apply or modify this idea to fit our situation?

#5   How do we know if we have really learnt from this?

#6   What are some best practices to adopt?

#7   Which areas can we apply this idea?

#8   ....

     ....

#9   ....

     ....

#10 ....

     ....

#11 ....

     ....

#12 ....

3.

Assessing Solutions

#1 On a scale of 1 to 10, how satisfied are you with the solution?

#2 How would those who disagree with this solution argue their case?

#3 What problems would this solution likely create?

#4 What might go wrong in the implementation of the solution?

#5   Would there be resistance? If so, how would you handle it?

#6   What are the metrics to measure the success of our solution?

#7   How long can this solution last?

#8   ....

    ....

#9   ....

    ....

#10 ....

    ....

#11 ....

    ....

#12 ....

4.

Building Rapport

#1   How are you?

#2   What can you tell me about yourself?

#3   What brings you here?

#4   What do you like about this place?

#5   How can I help?

#6   What do you need?

#7   What would interest you?

#8   ....

     ....

#9   ....

     ....

#10 ....

     ....

#11 ....

     ....

#12 ....

5.

Building Relationships

#1   How do I build a relationship with him?

#2   How can I be more approachable?

#3   How can we complement each other?

#4   How can we build a partnership?

#5   What is the basis of the relationship?

#6   How do you build trust in the relationship?

#7   How can we bring the relationship to the
     next level?

#8   ....

     ....

#9   ....

     ....

#10 ....

     ....

#11 ....

     ....

#12 ....

6.

Clarifying

#1   Am I right to say that you meant...?

#2   What I heard you say was... Was that what you meant?

#3   What should I write on the flipchart?

#4   Correct me if I am wrong. You were saying...?

#5 Can you rephrase what you have said in one sentence?

#6 What do you mean by...?

#7 Can you explain your point in a way that a six-year-old is able to understand?

#8 ....

....

#9 ....

....

#10 ....

....

#11 ....

....

#12 ....

7.

Clearing
the Air

#1   What is bothering you?

#2   Can we be honest with one another?

#3   How can we be open to one another?

#4   Can I be honest with you?

#5   Can you help me understand your situation?

#6   What is the real problem?

#7   What can I say to help you understand?

#8   ....

     ....

#9   ....

     ....

#10 ....

     ....

#11 ....

     ....

#12 ....

8.

Dealing with Ambiguity

#1   What are we confused about?

#2   How can we make this a "yes-and" situation?

#3   How do we take advantage of this situation?

#4   Who/What can enlighten us?

#5   How can we make sense of this?

#6   How can we live with the ambiguity?

#7   How can we make this a positive outcome?

#8   ....

      ....

#9   ....

      ....

#10   ....

      ....

#11   ....

      ....

#12   ....

9.

Dealing with Paradox

#1   How can I have the cake and eat it?

#2   How do I deal with this opposing view?

#3   Between the two, which is more important to me?

#4   How can I manage this and keep my sanity?

#5 What if there were no paradox?

#6 How can I deal with paradox?

#7 Who can help me see this situation better?

#8 ....

    ....

#9 ....

    ....

#10 ....

    ....

#11 ....

    ....

#12 ....

10.
Debriefing

#1   What did you take away from this?

#2   How do you feel about it?

#3   What worked and did not work just now?

#4   What were the key success factors?

#5   How can we not repeat this?

#6   What can we learn from this?

#7   What would you do differently?

#8   ....

      ....

#9   ....

      ....

#10   ....

      ....

#11   ....

      ....

#12   ....

11.

Delegating

#1 Who can best perform this task?

#2 Who would benefit from doing this?

#3 How can we make this a mentoring opportunity?

#4 What are the risks in delegating this?

#5   How can we mitigate the risk from delegating this?

#6   How much autonomy does the person have?

#7   Who is accountable for what?

#8   ....

....

#9   ....

....

#10 ....

....

#11 ....

....

#12 ....

12.

Delivering Presentations

#1   Do I have too many points on the slides?

#2   How do you engage the participants?

#3   How interactive would the presentation be?

#4   What are the key messages that you want to deliver?

#5 How do I make use of the physical space around me?

#6 How can I connect with the participants?

#7 How do I want the participants to feel after the presentation?

#8 ....

....

#9 ....

....

#10 ....

....

#11 ....

....

#12 ....

13.
Developing Careers

#1   What are your interests in life?

#2   What are your personal strengths?

#3   What do you not want to do?

#4   Given a choice, what would you prefer to do?

#5   What kind of work gives you energy and life?

#6   Who do you need to consider when contemplating a career switch?

#7   What drives you?

#8   ....

....

#9   ....

....

#10 ....

....

#11 ....

....

#12 ....

14.
Diffusing Tensions

#1   How can we take this down a notch?

#2   How are we feeling right now?

#3   Is this what we really want?

#4   What is happening to us now?

#5   How can we reduce this tension?

#6   What happens if we continue like this?

#7   Do we need a time-out?

#8 ....

....

#9 ....

....

#10 ....

....

#11 ....

....

#12 ....

15.

Driving Convergence

#1   What are the criteria for decision-making?

#2   What are our top three choices?

#3   If I were to force you to make a decision, what would you choose?

#4   How do we decide between choices?

#5   What are the low-hanging fruits?

#6   What is urgent and important?

#7   What is the decision-making process?

#8   ....

     ....

#9   ....

     ....

#10 ....

     ....

#11 ....

     ....

#12 ....

16.
Eliciting
Responses

#1 What do you think?

#2 What is going through your mind now?

#3 What would put you at ease to share your thoughts?

#4 Should I rephrase my question?

#5   Care to share your thoughts?

#6   How can I make it safe for you to share?

#7   What is holding you back?

#8   ....

....

#9   ....

....

#10 ....

....

#11 ....

....

#12 ....

17.

Enabling Actions

#1 What actions would you be taking?

#2 What are your next steps?

#3 What is the first thing that you would do?

#4 How would you carry out your tasks?

#5   Who can help you with these actions?

#6   What are the three things that you would do?

#7   What do you need to prepare?

#8   ....

     ....

#9   ....

     ....

#10 ....

     ....

#11 ....

     ....

#12 ....

18.

Encouraging Divergence

#1   What are our options?

#2   What else can we think of?

#3   What ideas do you have?

#4   What are the possibilities?

#5   What have we not thought of?

#6   What have we not tried so far?

#7   Can everyone come up with a different idea?

#8 ....

....

#9 ....

....

#10 ....

....

#11 ....

....

#12 ....

19.

Engaging the Client

#1   What are your concerns?

#2   What are your bottom lines?

#3   Are you open to new ideas?

#4   What are your constraints?

#5   How can I support you?

#6   What does success look like to you?

#7   How are you also part of the problem?

#8   ....

....

#9   ....

....

#10 ....

....

#11 ....

....

#12 ....

20.

Empowering Others

#1   How can you take charge of the situation?

#2   What can you do about it?

#3   What is stopping you?

#4   What are you in control of?

#5 Why are you limiting yourself?

#6 How can you get what you need?

#7 Who can support you?

#8 ....

    ....

#9 ....

    ....

#10 ....

    ....

#11 ....

    ....

#12 ....

21.

Gaining Commitment

#1   On a scale of 1 to 10, what is our commitment level?

#2   What would it take to increase our level of commitment?

#3   What are we committed to?

#4   What would cause our commitment to waver?

#5   What are we willing to do in order to demonstrate
     our commitment?

#6   How long would our commitment last?

#7   What is my personal commitment to this?

#8   ....

     ....

#9   ....

     ....

#10 ....

     ....

#11 ....

     ....

#12 ....

22.

Getting
Closure

#1   What is the conclusion?

#2   How do we put a close to this?

#3   What can we do to put a close to this?

#4   What must we do so that we do not have
        to discuss this again?

#5   How do we get closure from this?

#6   What must we do to put an end to this?

#7   How committed are we to end this once and for all?

#8   ....

      ....

#9   ....

      ....

#10   ....

      ....

#11   ....

      ....

#12   ....

23.

Getting Unstuck

#1   Why are we back here again?

#2   Can we retrace our steps?

#3   What led us to this situation?

#4   How can we prevent ourselves from getting stuck again?

#5   What should we do if we were to get stuck
      again?

#6   What is preventing us from moving forward?

#7   How can we help one another to get unstuck?

#8   ....

      ....

#9   ....

      ....

#10   ....

      ....

#11   ....

      ....

#12   ....

24.

Giving Feedback

#1   What did you do well?

#2   How can you do better?

#3   What are some areas of improvement?

#4   If you could do it again, what would you change?

#5   What were you happy with?

#6   What were you disappointed with?

#7   How do you think you did?

#8 ....

....

#9 ....

....

#10 ....

....

#11 ....

....

#12 ....

25.

Handling
Concerns

#1   You must have a reason for that. Do you mind
     if I ask you what it is?

#2   What can be done to address your concerns?

#3   What triggered such a strong reaction from
     you?

#4   What other information do you need?

#5 How can we work together in order to move forward?

#6 What can I do to help in this situation?

#7 What is the one thing that would help change your mind?

#8 ....

....

#9 ....

....

#10 ....

....

#11 ....

....

#12 ....

26.

Handling Objections

#1   What if what I said turned out to be true?

#2   What would make you say "yes"?

#3   What can I do to convince you?

#4   What is your real concern?

#5   What if there were a better way?

#6   What if there were a way to overcome your concerns?

#7   How can I better understand your concerns?

#8 ....

....

#9 ....

....

#10 ....

....

#11 ....

....

#12 ....

27.

Influencing
Others

#1   Do you know where they are coming from?

#2   What is the best way to win them over?

#3   How can you address their concerns?

#4   What would help them see from your point
      of view?

#5   Have you figured out their hidden concerns?

#6   What would enable them to come around?

#7   Have you understood them first?

#8   ....

      ....

#9   ....

      ....

#10   ....

      ....

#11   ....

      ....

#12   ....

28.

Making Connections

#1   What do we agree on?

#2   What is drawing us together?

#3   Where do we connect?

#4   Are you seeing what I am seeing?

#5   How are we joining the dots?

#6   How is this related to...?

#7   How can we make sense of these?

#8   ....

    ....

#9   ....

    ....

#10 ....

    ....

#11 ....

    ....

#12 ....

29.

Making
Observations

#1   What am I seeing?

#2   What am I noticing?

#3   Is my observation clouded by my mental model?

#4   Am I being objective in my observations?

#5 Am I seeing or interpreting?

#6 Who else is seeing what I see?

#7 Am I focussing on the behaviours or intentions?

#8 ....

....

#9 ....

....

#10 ....

....

#11 ....

....

#12 ....

30.

Making Personal Change

#1   What do I want to achieve?

#2   What are my choices?

#3   What assumptions am I making?

#4   What am I responsible for?

#5   What questions should I be asking?

#6   Why do I want to make this change?

#7   How can I move forward?

#8 ....

....

#9 ....

....

#10 ....

....

#11 ....

....

#12 ....

31.

Managing Change

#1 What would it take to obtain buy-in from stakeholders?

#2 What is the business case for change?

#3 What are the processes and systems that require change?

#4 Who can prevent the change?

#5   Who can we rely on to make the change happen?

#6   How do we get everyone on board?

#7   What is our communications plan?

#8 ....

....

#9 ....

....

#10 ....

....

#11 ....

....

#12 ....

32.

Moving Forward

#1   How can we move forward?

#2   What suggestions do you have on our next
     step?

#3   If we could do it all over again, what would
     we do?

#4   How can we have a happy ending?

#5 What challenges do we need to overcome?

#6 What is holding us back?

#7 What do you need from me to take the next
    step?

#8 ....

    ....

#9 ....

    ....

#10 ....

    ....

#11 ....

    ....

#12 ....

33.

Organising

#1   Have I covered all bases?

#2   What is the timeline?

#3   Does everyone know who is responsible for what?

#4   What is the plan?

#5   What is the back-up plan?

#6   When do we have a review?

#7   What are the possible failure points?

#8   ....

....

#9   ....

....

#10   ....

....

#11   ....

....

#12   ....

34.

Practising Open Communication

#1   Do you have an open-door policy?

#2   Are you open to feedback and suggestions?

#3   Are you asking good questions?

#4   How do you practise two-way communication?

#5   Do you judge ideas too quickly?

#6   When was the last time you asked for feedback
on your communication style?

#7   How often do you communicate?

#8 ....

....

#9 ....

....

#10 ....

....

#11 ....

....

#12 ....

35.

Probing for Clarification

#1 What do you mean by...?

#2 Can you elaborate on what you have just said?

#3 When you said..., do you mean...?

#4 What assumptions did you make when you said that?

#5   What was on your mind when you said...?

#6   How is what you have said related to the
     question I asked?

#7   Could you give me an example?

#8   ....

     ....

#9   ....

     ....

#10 ....

     ....

#11 ....

     ....

#12 ....

36.
Problem-Solving

#1   What is the problem?

#2   What are the root causes?

#3   What data and evidence do we have?

#4   Who can help us solve this?

#5   What can we do to eradicate this once and for all?

#6   What is the long-term solution?

#7   What problems would this solution create?

#8   ....

....

#9   ....

....

#10 ....

....

#11 ....

....

#12 ....

37.
Provoking Action

#1   Who is not trying hard enough?

#2   What are we avoiding?

#3   What are we not doing?

#4   What is stopping us from taking action?

#5   There must be another way. What is it?

#6   Why are we back here again?

#7   What is our problem?

#8   ....

     ....

#9   ....

     ....

#10 ....

     ....

#11 ....

     ....

#12 ....

38.

Reframing

#1   What can we learn from this?

#2   What could the other person be thinking?

#3   What am I not seeing?

#4   How can this be a good thing for me?

#5 How can we see it from his point of view?

#6 How can we look at this from another angle?

#7 How can I be better at doing this?

#8 ....

....

#9 ....

....

#10 ....

....

#11 ....

....

#12 ....

39.
Seeking Purpose

#1   Why are we here?

#2   What is the purpose?

#3   What are we focussing on?

#4   What are the core issues?

#5 Why is this important?

#6 What are we trying to achieve?

#7 What problem are we trying to solve?

#8 ....

....

#9 ....

....

#10 ....

....

#11 ....

....

#12 ....

40.

Setting Goals

#1   What is our goal?

#2   Can we consider the S.M.A.R.T. goals?

#3   How realistic are our goals?

#4   What are we trying to achieve?

#5   When would we know that we have achieved
     our goal?

#6   Does everyone have the same goal in mind?

#7   Has our goal changed?

#8   ....

     ....

#9   ....

     ....

#10 ....

     ....

#11 ....

     ....

#12 ....

41.
Setting Priorities

#1   What is most important?

#2   What are the top three priorities?

#3   Have we got our priorities sorted out?

#4   What are the things that can be easily done?

#5   What is our end game?

#6   What matters most?

#7   What is our first step?

#8 ....

....

#9 ....

....

#10 ....

....

#11 ....

....

#12 ....

42.

Speaking Effectively

#1   Am I speaking in long sentences?

#2   How can I make my sentences succinct?

#3   Do I know his preferred communication style?

#4   Besides speaking, what other forms of communication appeal to the audience?

#5   Am I asking enough questions?

#6   Am I relaxed and speaking clearly?

#7   Am I clear about the message I want to convey?

#8   ....

      ....

#9   ....

      ....

#10   ....

      ....

#11   ....

      ....

#12   ....

43.

Staying Focussed

#1   How close are we to the outcome?

#2   Can we direct ourselves back to the issue?

#3   Are we still on track?

#4   Where are we heading now?

#5   What can we do to stay on track?

#6   Where did we spend our energy on in the past
     x minutes?

#7   How can we put all the wood behind the arrow?

#8   ....

     ....

#9   ....

     ....

#10 ....

     ....

#11 ....

     ....

#12 ....

44.

Synthesising
Ideas

#1   What are some of the common themes we have uncovered?

#2   What are some of the things that you keep hearing?

#3   Which idea stands out for you?

#4   What is missing in the presentation?

#5   What keeps appearing?

#6   What are some similarities?

#7   What conclusions can we draw from this?

#8   ....

     ....

#9   ....

     ....

#10 ....

     ....

#11 ....

     ....

#12 ....

45.

Understanding the Client

#1 What does the client really need?

#2 What is he not saying?

#3 What are his constraints?

#4 How can I better understand the client?

#5   How does the client view me?

#6   How can I convince him to trust me?

#7   How much information does he need from me?

#8   ....

     ....

#9   ....

     ....

#10 ....

     ....

#11 ....

     ....

#12 ....

AFTERWORD

> **"** The power to question is the basis of
> all human progress. **"**
> *Indira Gandhi*

A good question is one that provokes more questions. I hope you have used the space in the pages to pen down your questions and reflections.

Learning certainly does not stop here—this is just the start of an on-going journey. Essentially, the inquiring mindset is the habit, curiosity and courage of asking open-minded questions of ourselves and others.

To support you in your learning journey, I would like to send you a list of 100 self-reflection questions. All you need to do is send me an email at **whatsyourquestion@idialogue.sg** and share with me how this book has helped you, or the questions that had been most useful to you.

It is my hope that this book ignites your spirit of inquiry. You can also explore developmental programmes that are offered by Inquiring Dialogue and the World Institute for Action Learning (WIAL).

REFERENCES

Adams, Marilee. *Change Your Questions, Change Your Life.* New York: Berret-Koehler, 2004.

Allen, David and Tina Blythe. *The Facilitator's Book of Questions.* New York: Teachers College Press, 2004.

Alvarado, Amy Edmonds and Patricia Herr. *Inquiry-Based Learning.* Thousand Oaks, 2003.

Bannink, Frederike. *1001 Solution-Focused Questions.* New York, W.W. Norton, 2006.

Barber, Judy. *Good Question! The Art of Asking Questions to Bring Positive Change.* Georgia: Bookshaker, 2005.

Brown, Neil M. and Stuart M. Keeley. *Asking the Right Questions: A Guide to Critical Thinking.* New Jersey: Prentice Hall, 2007.

Clark-Epstein, Chris. *78 Important Questions Every Leader Should Ask and Answer.* New York: Amacom, 2002.

Cooper, Ian. *Just Ask the Right Questions to Get What You Want.* Harlow: Pearson Education Limited, 2007.

Dantonia, Marylou and Paul C. Beisenherz. *Learning to Question, Question to Learn.* Needham Heights: Allyn & Bacon, 2001.

Dark, David. *The Sacredness of Questioning Everything.* Grand Rapids: Zondervan, 2009.

Facilitator Question Collections. Arroyo Grande: FacilitatorU.com, 2007.

Fadem, Terry J. *The Art of Asking.* New Jersey: FT Press, 2008.

Falk Beverly and Megan Blumenreich. *The Power of Questions.* Portsmouth: Heinemann, 2005.

Finlayson, Andrew. *Questions That Work.* New York: Amacom, 2008.

Fisco, Esther. *Effective Questioning Strategies in the Classroom.* New York: Teachers College Press, 2012.

Flage, Daniel E. *The Art of Questioning: An Introduction to Critical Thinking.* New Jersey: Prentice Hall, 2004.

Freed, Alice F. and Susan Ehrlich. *Why Do You Ask?* New York: Oxford, 2010.

Freese, Thomas A. *Secrets of Questions Based Selling.* Naperville: Sourcebooks Inc., 2003.

Frischknecht, Jacqueline and EllaMarie Schroeder. *Asking Smart Questions.* Marion: Pieces of Learning, 2006.

Fry, Ron. *Asking the Right Questions, Hire the Best People.* Franklin Lakes: Career Press, 2006.

Gschwandtner, Gerhard. *Sales Questions That Closes Every Deal.* San Francisco: McGraw-Hill Education, 2007.

Koechlin, Carol and Sandi Zwaan. *Q Tasks: How to Empower Students to Ask Questions and Care about Answers.* Ontario: Prembroke Publishers, 2007.

Leeds, Dorothy. *Smart Questions: The Essential Strategy for Successful Managers.* New York: Berkley Publishing, 2000.

Leeds, Dorothy. *The 7 Powers of Questions.* New York: Penguin Group, 2000.

Marquardt, Michael J. *Action Learning in Action: Transforming Problems and People for World-Class Organizational Learning.* Mountain View: Davies-Black Publishing, 1999.

Marquardt, Michael J. *Optimizing the Power of Action Learning: Solving Problems and Building Leaders in Real Time.* Mountain View: Davies-Black Publishing. 2004.

Marquardt, Michael J. *Action Learning for Developing Leaders and Organizations: Principles, Strategies, and Cases.* Washington DC: APA Press, 2009.

Marquardt, Michael J. *Leading with Questions: How Leaders Find the Right Solutions by Knowing What to Ask.* San Francisco: Jossey Bass, 2005.

Maxwell, John. *Good Leaders Ask Great Questions.* New York: Hachette, 2014.

McKenzie, Jamie. *Leading Questions.* Bellington: FNO Press, 2007.

McKenzie, Jamie. *Learning to Question to Wonder to Learn.* Bellington: FNO Press, 2005.

McTighe, Jay and Grant Wiggins. *Essential Questions: Opening Doors to Student Understanding.* Alexandria: ASCD, 2013.

Miller, John G. *The Question behind the Question.* New York: G.P. Putnam's Sons, 2001.

Morgan, Norah and Juliana Saxton. *Asking Better Questions.* Ontario: Prembroke Publishers, 2006.

Norden-Powers, Christo. *Powerful Questions that Highly Effective Business Leaders Ask.* Victoria: Spandah Pte Ltd, 2010.

Peery, Angela, Polly Patrick and Deb Moore. *Ask, Don't Tell: Powerful Questioning in the Classroom.* Englewood: Lead & Learn Press, 2013.

Poole, Garry D. *The Complete Book of Questions.* Willow Creek: Zondervan, 2003.

Short, Kathy G. *Learning Together through Inquiry.* Maine: Stenhouse, 1996.

Stock, Gregory. *The Book of Questions.* New York: Workman Publishing, 1987.

Stoltzfus, Tony. *Coaching Questions: A Coach's Guide to Powerful Asking Skills.* Virginia Beach:

Strachan, Dorothy. *Making Questions Work: A Guide to What and How to Ask for Facilitators, Consultants, Managers, Coaches and Educators*. San Francisco: Jossey Bass, 2007.

Walsh, Jackie A. and Beth D. Sattes. *Quality Questioning: Research-Based Practice to Engage Every Learning*. London: Sage, 2005.

Walsh, Jackie A. and Beth D. Sattes. *Leading through Quality Questioning*. London: Sage, 2010.

Weinbaum, Alexandra, David Allen, Tina Blythe, et al. *Teaching as Inquiry*. Oxford: National Staff Development Council, 2004.

Whitney, Diana, Amanda Trosten-Bloom, David Cooperrider, et al. *Encyclopedia of Positive Questions*. Brunswick: Crown Custom Publishing, 2005.

Wilson, Rainn, Devon Gundry, Golriz Lucina, et al. *Soul Pancake: Chew on Life's Big Questions*. New York: Hyperion, 2010.

ABOUT THE AUTHOR

In the past 25 years, Ng Choon Seng has made significant impact in the world of professional and organisational development. Equipped with a vast wealth of knowledge, Choon Seng has experience in leading the learning & development and human resource functions in the hospitality and manufacturing sectors. He has also led and managed organisation development in Fortune 500 companies, including the Corporate University for Sun Microsystems in Asia South.

Choon Seng is one of the first in Singapore to be an International Association of Facilitators (IAF) Certified Professional Facilitator (CPF), and the first Singaporean to be certified as an IAF CPF Assessor in 2006. He is also the only Singaporean to be certified by the World Institute for Action Learning (WIAL) as a Certified Master Action Learning Coach. He helms the role of Principal Master Facilitator for the Power of Questions

Choon Seng received his Masters of Arts in Human Resource Development (MAHRD) from George Washington University (GWU) and was awarded the Leonard Nadler Leadership Award for his outstanding leadership, service, professional, and academic successes. Choon Seng is the co-author of two peer-reviewed articles titled "Team Development via Action Learning" published by the Academy of Human Resources Development (AHRD), and "Consulting in International Context" published by the American Psychological Association.

Choon Seng is the designer and developer of the popular "Power of Questions Dialogue Cards", a set of powerful questioning cards to help people engage in deep and meaningful conversations. The cards can be purchased online at www.facilitationstore.com.

He leads his own facilitation and coaching practice under Inquiring Dialogue Pte Ltd. (www.idialogue.sg), and is also the Managing Director of WIAL Singapore (www.wial.sg).

THE POWER OF QUESTIONS™ Series

The Power of Questions Dialogue Cards

The Power of Questions Dialogue Cards is available in two volumes of 100 cards each. Each card contains an interesting and thought-provoking question that is ideal for creating deep conversation. With endless possibilities, this is a great activity for networking sessions, coaching conversations and icebreakers.

The Power of Questions Workshop

This is a 1-day interactive questioning skills workshop to enable you to ask good questions using different questioning frameworks. You will find what you learned applicable in both your professional and personal life.

What's Your Question?: Inspiring Possibilities through the Power of Questions

This book is a compilation of 630 questions grouped under two categories—Situations and Competencies. A handy resource for anyone who is keen in asking better questions in different contexts.

For more information, visit

Made in United States
Orlando, FL
05 July 2023

34762222R00133